The Praying Writer

Prayers & Scripture
for the Writing Process

Carol Peterson

Honor Bound Books

Honor Bound Books

ISBN-13: 978-0692641873
ISBN-10: 0692641874

Dedication

This book is dedicated to writers whose ministry it is to use their skill with the written word to honor God and point others to Him.

Contents

The Praying Writer

Prayers & Scripture
for the Writing Process

Praying for Our Writing

~

Some days writing is a joy, filled with brilliant, sparkling stars. Other days we feel trapped in a pit so deep we wonder if stars even exist out there.

Fortunately, God is with us always—whether star gazing or holding us as we sit in the pit. As Christian writers, our purpose is to shine the light of Christ into the world, so others might see that light and walk toward it. Despite our lofty goal to honor God, sometimes we begin and complete projects without stopping and praying as the very first and most important part of the writing process.

As writers, we know that the process of creating something to be read by others contains many, very different aspects. Some parts of writing require inspiration, others require courage or humility or submission to others.

Praying for our Writing

The Holy Spirit, living right here inside of us knows what we are going through and understands what we need in order to accomplish the tasks of each aspect of writing.

The prayers in this book are meant to help writers call upon the Holy Spirit during whatever part of the writing process we are in. The accompanying Scripture is a reminder of God's promises in our writing lives.

May you be blessed and bless others through the words you string together.

Learning the Craft

Writing is a skill. Yes, there must be ability, talent even, but it is also something that can be learned and improved upon. Sometimes that process of learning, involves unlearning what we think we know or what we have been doing incorrectly or not well. Sometimes the process of learning requires us to be honest enough to recognize our weakness and humble enough to accept the guidance and teaching of others.

Through it all, learning requires practice and patience as we master new skills we have available to make our writing better.

Scripture

~

The fear of the Lord is the beginning of knowledge, but fools despise wisdom and instruction (Proverbs 1:7).

Prayer

~

Dear Jesus, some days we truly think we know what we are doing. Some days we even think we know it all, when it comes to writing. Each time we sit down to write, please humble us and open our eyes to see something we might be able to do differently or better.

Please keep us seeking to increase our knowledge and skill in the craft of writing. More importantly, please keep us seeking to increase our knowledge and understanding of you. Amen.

Notes, Questions & Prompts

What area of writing do I feel most confident in?

What area of writing do I feel unsure of?

Who do I know who might help me learn?

Who might I be able to help learn what I know?

What one step can I do today to help myself with this issue?

What I want to remember about this writing issue:

Inspiration

Each writing project begins with an idea. Some ideas are only developed through hard work. Some ideas come seemingly through the ether floating down from heaven on angel wings. Sometimes we have to chase down inspiration, beat it up and force it into submission before we can take the inspiration and move it toward a work of writing.

However we capture inspiration, it is an essential part of the writing process—whether from the inception of the idea or at the end of the project, when the inspiration has become a clear reality.

Scripture

~

But when he, the Spirit of truth, comes, he will guide you into all the truth. He will not speak on his own; he will speak only what he hears, and he will tell you what is yet to come (John 16:13).

Prayer

Dear Jesus, thank you for this world and everything in it. Thank you that inspiration surrounds us. Holy Spirit, please open our eyes to see the inspiration. And please remind us that inspiration is only the beginning of the process of developing a work of writing.

Remind us, Spirit, that what takes us from inspiration to finished work is the sitting and doing. Please help us sit patiently and do the work necessary to create the writing that will glorify you. Amen.

Notes, Questions & Prompts

Where do I usually find inspiration?

Have I prayed for inspiration? Do I need to pray again?

Have I tried sitting down and writing while awaiting inspiration?

What I want to remember about this writing issue:

Brainstorming Ideas

∾

Many writers claim that forces seemingly outside their own minds appear to be in charge of their projects. Other times we feel like we've come to a dead end of an argument or plot line or character development. During those times, we recognize that our project could develop in multiple possible directions.

Which direction would be best for a particular project? What direction might be better than any I am considering right now? How can I generate ideas to take my own writing—or the writing of a colleague I want to help—to make it better?

Scripture

~

Finally, brothers and sisters, whatever is true, whatever is noble, whatever is right, whatever is pure, whatever is lovely, whatever is admirable—if anything is excellent or praiseworthy—think about such things. Whatever you have learned or received or heard from me, or seen in me—put it into practice. And the God of peace will be with you (Philippians 4:8-9).

Prayer

～

Dear Jesus, with some projects, we know exactly what we want to say and how to say it. We clearly see how to organize our words to lead our readers from here to there. Other days we feel stuck in one spot. We spin in circles, not knowing which direction to take, not having ideas to lead our readers onward.

When that happens, Holy Spirit, please clear our minds and open them to what we have not seen before. Help us focus on what is true, noble, right, pure, lovely, admirable, excellent or praiseworthy. Let Paul's words remind us that our brains need not focus so tightly on what we might have previously thought that we are unable to see new directions our work might take.

Through it all, please help us find ways to honor you. Amen.

Notes, Questions & Prompts

What questions do I need to ask my characters?

What questions might my readers be asking?

What is the next logical step? Should I follow the next logical step or is another way better?

What I want to remember about this writing issue:

Outlining and Planning

Many writers are "pantsters." They write by the seat of their pants, ignoring attempts at planning. Others of us can't write a word unless we know clearly our starting point, where we are headed and how we intend to get there.

But even "pantsters" need to plan at some point, to help them keep track of elements of their work and make sure they are covering all issues that need to be addressed.

Scripture

~

"Suppose one of you wants to build a tower. Won't you first sit down and estimate the cost to see if you have enough money to complete it?" (Luke 14:28).

Prayer

Dear Jesus, thank you so much for ideas. Many times, we become inspired and sit down and write, write, write, the words flowing from point to point and scene to scene seamlessly.

But those times of inspiration are not usually the norm and most often we need to spend time thinking about where our work begins and what needs to be written to flesh out ideas, characters, themes or circumstances so that the concluding point or story makes sense and is satisfying to our reader.

When those times of needed planning occur, please be with us, Holy Spirit and guide our minds and hands. Please show us ways to begin our works and bring our readers with us as we create projects that will honor you. Amen.

Notes, Questions & Prompts

Do I know where my project is going—the end result?

Do I know how to get there?

Is there one logical approach to the ending?

Is there a better way to organize my material? Chronological? Thematic? Circular?

What I want to remember about this writing issue:

Permission to Write Badly

~

Early drafts are horrible. Their purpose is to get everything—theme, character, background, plot elements, setting—out of our heads and into a document. They clear our brains and allow us to see the information visually.

Once in a document, facts and background issues can be organized. What should be deleted can be placed to one side for reference. What remains that is not yet good, but essential can be reworked and revised. It is not just allowable to write bad drafts, it is a writer's duty to do so, so that what is nonessential can be cast aside and what is important can be made beautiful.

Scripture

~

He has made everything beautiful in its time. He has also set eternity in the human heart; yet no one can fathom what God has done from beginning to end (Ecclesiastes 3:11).

Prayer

~

Dear Jesus, thank you for giving us life. Thank you even more for taking us as we are and working in our hearts to turn us into something beautiful. Thank you that you do the same with all of our circumstances.

In our writing, please remind us what you are doing in our lives. Remind us that, as writers, we have permission—and are expected—to write horrible drafts in order to get the ideas out of our heads and into a document where they can be sorted and organized. Remind us that we can take our horrible drafts and work on them to turn them into something beautiful, like you are doing with us.

Help us not be discouraged by early drafts, but keep in mind that it takes time—even for you—to turn things into something beautiful. Amen.

Notes, Questions & Prompts

Have I embraced the truth that a first draft is supposed to be horrible?

How can I release my fear that my first draft will never get better?

Have I determined what information in my first draft needs to stay and what was written for my own benefit?

Out of the information that needs to remain, what needs to be filtered into the book later? Where? How?

What I want to remember about this writing issue:

Research

~

Whether we write fiction or non-fiction often we need to research. Sometimes we need to understand concepts or facts so that our interpretation can be clear. Sometimes we need to understand points of view so that our arguments can be strengthened. Sometimes we need to understand locations or science for creating settings or characters, memorable to our readers.

Often the research is interesting, inspiring us in new directions or giving us confidence of the way we should go. Other times, the research feels like we are spinning in circles and heading in too many directions, compiling too many facts and not making sense of anything. During those times, we sometimes just need to dig in and gather the information to help create the work we see in our imaginations.

Scripture

~

Of making many books there is no end, and much study wearies the body (Ecclesiastes 12:12).

Prayer

~

Dear Jesus, thank you for our minds. Thank you also for the ability to use words to convey messages, set scenes and share facts with our readers.

Some days, our research takes us into areas where we are enlivened and excited to share what we have learned with our readers. Other times, our research feels like a millstone around our necks.

Please remind us that when we feel weary from the research, that the ultimate goal is to be obedient to you in our writing. During those times, please lighten our spirit and help us regain the excitement needed to eagerly share our research with others. Amen.

Notes, Questions & Prompts

What facts, figures, history, culture, science do I need to know?

Have I taken into account alternative lines of thinking? Arguments? Points of view? Do I need to?

What research would make my writing richer?

What I want to remember about this writing issue:

Drudgery

Sometimes our writing is a roller coaster of fun. Other times we drag a sentence from our brains one painful word at a time. Sometimes the drudgery of our work involves making sure each punctuation point is proper or that words are capitalized consistently throughout our 150,000 word story.

Parts of writing may involve drudgery, but they are important parts of the writing process because they enable our reader to painlessly reach the end of our work; maybe even with joy.

Scripture

~

Strengthen the feeble hands, steady the knees that give way (Isaiah 35:3).

Prayer

~

Jesus, thank you for the opportunity to write. Some days the process of arranging words is exciting and satisfying. They seem to fly from our brains, through our fingers and onto paper as if by magic. But other days, we feel as if the words are hiding amid gray and bulbous brain cells that are barely functioning.

On those days, Holy Spirit, please encourage us. Remind us that you have given us this talent for creating stories and explaining truths to the world. Remind us, Jesus of your creation and that hard work is necessary in order to create something worthy. Thank you for the stamina and strength you give us to complete our projects. Amen.

Notes, Questions & Prompts

How can I break down the process? Can I first go through the document looking at punctuation? Then spelling? Then removing extra words (very, that, etc.)?

How can I use time productively so that I allow breaks without wasting time?

What other project can I work on between chunks of time needed?

What I want to remember about this writing issue:

Fleshing Out Our Work

~

We think each word is perfect. We praise our tight writing. We pat ourselves on the back for such a neat and tidy story line. Then we remember that our reader may need more explanation; maybe a one-sentence explanation is not enough. Perhaps our reader needs to experience the setting more fully. It is our job as presenter of words to make the writing fit the needs of our reader.

Sometimes that may even mean we need more words.

Scripture

~

Do your best to present yourself to God as one approved, a worker who does not need to be ashamed and who correctly handles the word of truth (2 Timothy 2:15).

Prayer

~

Dear Jesus, sometimes when we write, things seem so clear to us. Our stories move smoothly from chapter to chapter and scene to scene. We present an argument and rationally move from thesis through explanation to conclusion.

Remind us please though that our readers cannot see inside our heads and understand our points without explanation. Please guide our writing so that the themes and purposes of our writing are evident to our intended audience. Remind us always that we are writing to share your world with others; not to keep your world tightly held to our own hearts. Amen.

Notes, Questions & Prompts

Have I brainstormed and planned adequately?

Which sections stand by themselves?

Which sections feel slight?

What issues, arguments, facts, plot elements have I not addressed?

What I want to remember about this writing issue:

Organization of Material

~

There are many ways to organize material. Sometimes a linear argument is best. Other times, outside information may be required, interspersed between the linear.

In fiction, often backstory is needed to help the reader understand a character, but a sudden dump of information would threaten to entice a reader to set the book down and move to another. It is a writer's job to organize material in a way that moves a reader forward, turning pages from sentence to sentence, chapter to chapter and ultimately book to book.

Scripture

~

But everything should be done in a fitting and orderly way (1 Corinthians 14:40).

Prayer

Lord, we recognize the need for organization. We recognize that there are many ways our ideas and plot elements could be introduced to our readers. We recognize that some ways though might be better than others.

Help us discern the best organization for our projects so that—not our way—but our reader's and especially your way—is addressed. Amen.

Notes, Questions & Prompts

What elements feel out of place?

Where should they logically appear?

Is there a better way to present information?

Have I handled transitions appropriately to lead the reader easily?

What I want to remember about this writing issue:

Using Time Effectively

~

Writing advice says that a writer could draft a 50,000 word novel in one year by writing just 150 words a day. Sometimes though it is not a matter of finding time to write 150 words. It is a matter of being distracted by life and technology. It is a matter of focusing on making those 150 words of value. It is a matter of managing time effectively so that the writing becomes a priority.

Scripture

~

Teach us to number our days, that we may gain a heart of wisdom (Psalm 90:12).

Prayer

Jesus, thank you for creating time. We realize that the time we will have with you in Heaven will have no end. We are so grateful that you have included us in your plan for eternity.

We also want, however, to make the best use of our time here on earth to create works that honor you. When we are uncertain or afraid of the next step in our writing projects, sometimes we procrastinate. Sometimes we avoid doing what is needed by doing things that are not essential.

Please direct our minds so we can move forward, even if the words are not quite right or lovely, reminding us that we can return to them for revision later. Amen.

Notes, Questions & Prompts

What does my current writing time look like?

Do I need to focus on changing the time of day or location for writing?

Do I feel like I'm wasting time doing things that aren't necessary?

What is one thing I could do differently to better use my writing time?

What I want to remember about this writing issue:

Writer's Block

Writer's block can be caused by many things—distraction, procrastination, fear, lack of direction, fatigue, lack of confidence. Every writer encounters such times.

When that happens, the best thing to do is pray. Then sit down and write. Great words. Or drivel. But write. Expect the words to be bad. Then remember that they are words; we have a nearly endless supply of them and we absolutely do have an endless way in which they can be combined. They can be changed tomorrow; made clearer; made better; made good.

Scripture

~

Look to the Lord and his strength; seek his face always (1 Chronicles 16:11).

Prayer

~

Dear Jesus, some days we feel incapable of moving forward. We don't know how to get our characters through the obstacles we have placed in their way. We don't know how to introduce a theme or truth in a way that our readers will understand or accept.

We know our minds really aren't blocked; that there is a way out or through restrictions we place on ourselves. If our block is fear, please give us courage to try. If our block is uncertainty, remind us that to simply proceed is part of the process. If our block is because we lack direction, please give us leading from a friend or writing colleague. Remind us that the most important part of writing is showing up and placing the pen in our hands or our fingers on the keyboard.

And Jesus, if this block lasts longer than we hope, please give us patience and encouragement while we wait. Amen.

Notes, Questions & Prompts

What do I think is causing my block? Fear, uncertainty? Are my reasons for those emotions valid? Why or why not?

Do I recognize the truth that the words I write today can be made better tomorrow?

Can I simply sit down and write and plan to change the words tomorrow?

Is there another project I can work on until I unblock on this one?

What I want to remember about this writing issue:

The Creative Process

~

There is no one "right" creative process for writing. Each person has a way of writing that works for them and something that doesn't work. It may involve the physical tools we use to write. It may be a specific time of day or location that makes us more efficient. It may be how we write chapters or in what order.

Often it takes years to understand a person's individual process. It is the writer's duty though ultimately to discover that process and then to embrace it.

Scripture

~

In the beginning, God created the heavens and the earth. The earth was without form and void, and darkness was over the face of the deep. And the Spirit of God was hovering over the face of the waters. And God said, "Let there be light," and there was light. And God saw that the light was good. And God separated the light from the darkness. God called the light Day, and the darkness he called Night. And there was evening and there was morning, the first day (Genesis 1:1-31).

Prayer

Dear Jesus, through your example, remind us that we must create a universe before placing a world in it; must create an ocean before swimming creatures can survive in it. Remind us that we must first establish truths before we ask our readers to move to the next stage of an argument or conclusion.

Throughout the process, Holy Spirit, please encourage us. Remind us for whom we are writing—you first and our readers secondly. Remind us that as joyous as writing may be to us personally, you have gifted us for your purpose. Please remind us also that your creative process in our lives is ongoing and never ending. Amen.

Notes, Questions & Prompts

Do I understand my personal creative process?

Can I think through my process and write it down?

What is the first step in my process? The second? The third? The final step?

How might I improve my process?

What I want to remember about this writing issue:

Focusing on Readers

There is a bond between a writer and reader. It is the writer's duty to present an idea, argument, theme or story in a way that the reader's life will be better for having read it. The reader trusts the writer when he picks up the book and reads the first sentence.

The reader is opening his mind, spending his money, giving time and bringing that book into his home where his loved ones live. It is the writer's duty not to disappoint, but to make the reader's investment of value. A writer can only adequately do that when he first focuses on who his reader is and how his reader will benefit from reading his book.

Scripture

And let us consider how we may spur one another on toward love and good deeds (Hebrews 10:24).

Prayer

Dear Jesus, thank you for Scripture. Thank you that each person who penned the words contained in our Holy Bible knew that we readers needed to hear exactly what was recorded.

When we are writing, please help us keep our reader in our focus. Guide us in understanding the exact message our reader needs to hear. Help us present our words in a way that our reader will not only understand the message clearly but will embrace the truths enthusiastically.

In all of our writing, please show us ways to assure that you are honored and glorified. Amen.

Notes, Questions & Prompts

Do I clearly know who my readers are?

What are their ages?

Education?

Interests?

Am I addressing the above?

What I want to remember about this writing issue:

Finding Our Voice

~

Do we write like we speak? Do we write for a specific group of people? A specific age? Do we write in a way that our ideas and stories are clear and welcomed by our reader?

It is our duty as a writer to find the voice that will be most easily heard by our reader.

Scripture

The words of the reckless pierce like swords, but the tongue of the wise brings healing (Proverbs 12:18).

Prayer

~

Dear Jesus, thank you for words and the power they hold. Please remind us of the power we wield by the way we put words together.

When we write, please help us write with a voice for our readers. If we need to write for a specific audience, please help us not sound so sophisticated that our words make our readers feel inferior. If our audience is young, please help us write in a way that uplifts them and does not make them feel preached to.

If we are trying to share your truth with people who do not believe, please help us keep our words those that they would understand, without theological explanations they might not be ready to accept or understand. Help us use the voice our readers will find pleasing to their ears. Amen.

Notes, Questions & Prompts

What is my voice? Is it appropriate for my readers?

Do I need to change my voice for specific projects?

Am I writing in the proper genre for my voice?

What I want to remember about this writing issue:

Persuading our Readers

When we write non-fiction, we seek to inform our readers, to influence their thinking, to change or grow or become stronger. In our desire to share what we know, it is easy to forget where they are coming from, their beginning point of view or arguments they may have that we do not address.

Even fiction writers need to occasionally write non-fiction—submission letters, blog posts, interviews and marketing material. Throughout it all, we need to not just make our points but also recognize our reader's beginning perspective.

Scripture

~

His (Paul's) letters contain some things that are hard to understand, which ignorant and unstable people distort, as they do the other Scriptures, to their own destruction (2 Peter 3:16, explanation added).

Prayer

~

Dear Jesus, it is an awesome responsibility to try and educate others or explain or persuade others to our point of view. Please give us discernment as to the validity of our work and whether or not it is righteous in your eyes.

If what we have to say is honoring to you, please help us be able to present our thoughts clearly to others in a way they will accept. Most especially, help us use words that point others to you. Amen.

Notes, Questions & Prompts

Is the intention of my thesis clear to me?

What steps have I taken to persuade my reader?

Is it effective?

Have I left out any steps, facts or arguments?

What might make the persuasion clearer?

What I want to remember about this writing issue:

Elements of Fiction

~

Many elements go into creating a satisfying piece of fiction. A writer must use setting, theme, character development, plot, pacing, voice, dialogue, description, obstacles, crises, story arc and imagination to create a world that readers enjoy spending time in.

It can be difficult to juggle so many variables over which the writer has control and options.

Scripture

~

I saw heaven standing open and there before me was a white horse, whose rider is called Faithful and True. With justice he judges and wages war. His eyes are like blazing fire, and on his head are many crowns. He has a name written on him that no one knows but he himself (Revelation 19:11-12, as a biblical example of setting and description).

Prayer

Dear Jesus, we love stories. We love creating worlds and filling them with characters and circumstances that can inspire and entertain others. We understand what needs to be done to create stories that others will love. Sometimes the complexity of it all though seems overwhelming.

Please remind us, Jesus that you spoke in parables. Remind us that stories have power. Remind us that stories can make hard truths easier to understand and accept.

Please guide our hands as we create, Holy Spirit. Let our stories be pleasing to others. More importantly, let them be pleasing to you. Amen.

Notes, Questions & Prompts

Have I looked at character development?

Have I looked at plot?

Is my setting interesting?

How have I handled backstory?

Is my dialogue realistic?

Is my pacing appropriate?

What is my story arc?

What I want to remember about this writing issue:

Fear

Sometimes we are afraid. We are afraid that we can't bring justice to our lofty idea or story. We are afraid that our readers will reject what we have written. We are afraid that we are not up to the project.

The words we string together come from our hearts and our minds. They are dear to us. They are important. We want them to be important to others, too.

Scripture

~

There is no fear in love. But perfect love drives out fear, because fear has to do with punishment. The one who fears is not made perfect in love (1 John 4:18).

Prayer

~

Dear Jesus, in our minds, our writing is perfect and wonderful; it is flawless; it is of eternal importance. These lofty ideals sometimes make us afraid that we are not up to the job; that our projects will not be as beautiful as we envision them. We fear our readers will reject what we write. And—sometimes—we are afraid that what we write will disappoint you, Jesus.

Please remind us that fear is not from you. Remind us that when we are writing in obedience to you and following your guidance, even if the world sees what we write as of no value, it is pleasing to you because our hearts were right in the writing. Remind us that if only one person benefits from our writing, it is of eternal importance—even if that one person is us. Amen.

Notes, Questions & Prompts

Am I afraid of my readers' approval?

Am I afraid I can't do the work justice?

Am I afraid of publication?

What can I do to help get over my fear? Who do I know to encourage me?

What I want to remember about this writing issue:

Making it Good

~

Word by word; revision by revision—the work we create gets better. We look back at our first draft and name it appropriately: "horrible!"

But we celebrate in the process. We celebrate that we have taken an idea and have turned it into a work. We have expanded and explained, we have edited and revised. We have cut and added. And it is better. It is becoming "good!"

Scripture

~

God saw all that he had made, and it was very good
(Genesis 1:31).

Prayer

Jesus, thank you for creating this world and for declaring it very good. Lord, we too want what we create to be good. Sometimes we have difficulty knowing when we reach that point. Please give us discernment to know whether what we write needs improvement or whether we should declare it good and get it into the hands of readers who need to hear what we have to say.

When needed, please send colleagues into our lives who are able to discern where our writing needs more work. We would love all of our work to be perfect the first time but humbly admit that it usually isn't. Please give us understanding of our craft and the humble attitude to know when to continue on. Amen.

Notes, Questions & Prompts

What revision number am I on?

How many more revisions do I foresee?

Who else has read this work whose opinion I trust?

Do I agree with their comments? Why or why not?

Is the work getting better with each revisions? Or is it time to stop creating and declare it good?

What I want to remember about this writing issue:

Editing

Editing can be laborious. It can also be exhilarating. Editing is part of the process that takes a work from "done" to "great." But not only from our point of view.

Editing also must be done with the reader in mind. The goal is not only to create a work to be happy to call our own; but also to create a work for our reader to appreciate.

Scripture

~

...he who began a good work in you will carry it on to completion until the day of Christ Jesus (Philippians 1:6).

Prayer

~

Dear Jesus, thank you for being our editor in chief and for being in charge of the greatest book ever written.

Please remind us that we may get the big things—plot, characters, chapter order—right, but little details such as typos, punctuation, spacing between lines and font sizes become invisible when we have edited our work too long.

Holy Spirit you are so good at opening our spiritual eyes. Please open our physical eyes so we can also clearly see the editing needed. Help us make sure the writing we create is without blemish so that nothing would cause readers to discount the depth of the words we have to say; especially when those words are meant to point others to you. Amen.

Notes, Questions & Prompts

Do I clearly understand the editing process?

Is there an aspect of editing (grammar, spelling, punctuation, font choice and sizing, heading and chapter coordination, formatting) that I don't clearly understand?

Is there someone or somewhere I can go to in order to get the help I need?

What I want to remember about this writing issue:

Technology

~

We are fortunate to have the benefit of technology so that our work can more easily reach our readers. But sometimes that technology involves learning new processes that seem alien to our writer's mind.

Writing pieces to post online, submitting manuscripts electronically, creating websites, posting blogs, publishing independently often strain our brains and take us away from our much-loved desire to simply write.

Scripture

~

Then the Lord replied: "Write down the revelation and make it plain on tablets so that a herald may run with it (Habakkuk 2:2).

Prayer

~

Dear Jesus, we are so grateful for a way to record words for others to read. We are especially grateful to live in a time when technology allows us to get our writing to more people who may need to hear what we have to say. Thank you that we no longer have to write on a tablet and hire someone to run with it from town to town.

Sometimes though we are struck with the realization that the cyber world, word processing and technology in general are not one of the spiritual gifts you gave us. When that happens, we are frustrated or need wisdom or the help of a person who does have those gifts.

Please lead us to the help we need, whether finding colleagues who can assist us or leading us to the answers through learning. Then encourage us to pass that knowledge to other writers also struggling with technology. Amen.

Notes, Questions & Prompts

What aspects of technology do I not understand that I need to?

Where can I go to learn?

What's stopping me from learning?

Who can I help with the technology I do understand?

What I want to remember about this writing issue:

Networking

~

Many writers are self-proclaimed introverts. We are often happiest sitting alone in a room in front of a computer screen. But we must live in a world, even if we are not to live of the world. And one of the loveliest parts of being a writer is being able to be part of a writing community, sharing our love of writing and our experience with it.

Scripture

~

"For where two or three gather in my name, there am I with them" (Matthew 18:20).

Prayer

~

Dear Jesus, even though some days we think we are happiest sitting alone at our desk writing, we recognize that we need others. Please bring other writers who love you into our lives. Help us share our love of writing and our love of you with each other so that our writing and our faith are stronger.

Encourage us to attend workshops and conferences, critique groups and classes where we can grow our understanding of our craft. Help us share our knowledge and experience with others and open our minds to what we can learn from other writers who love you. Amen.

Notes, Questions & Prompts

Do I have other writing friends? Who might I know that needs a writing friend like me?

What writing conferences, classes and seminars happen near where I live?

What writing events and classes happen online that I could join?

What writing forums online might I join?

What I want to remember about this writing issue:

Submitting & Rejection

∼

When we write for publication, we must submit our work to the review of others. Even independently published writers or writers who only write on their personal websites, are still submitting their work to the world and being open to review and rejection. Submission can be a source of fear and uncertainty. Rejection hurts.

Scripture

Humble yourselves, therefore, under God's mighty hand, that he may lift you up in due time (1 Peter 5:6).

Prayer

~

Dear Jesus, sometimes, as much as we love what we have written; as much as we believe in what we have created, we fear how others will react to our words. Please remind us that others rejected you in the most horrifying way possible and that you took that rejection upon yourself for our benefit. Please help us use your example as a way to encourage our own strength.

And Jesus, when we submit our work to editors and agents and readers, should we encounter rejection of our work for publication, please remind us not to give up. Please remind us that other editors, agents and readers may not feel the same. Most importantly, please remind us that you will never reject us and that your love for us is forever. Amen.

Notes, Questions & Prompts

Am I pursuing traditional publishing?

If so, do I intend to submit my work to an agent? Which ones and why?

If so, do I intend to submit my work to an editor? Which ones and why?

If I intend to independently publish, where can I later submit my work for editing and review?

What I want to remember about this writing issue:

Celebrating Success

~

Sometimes we sell a book manuscript. Sometimes we just finish one. Sometimes we have an idea for a project. Or think of the perfect title. Or word. Whatever part of the writing process we are in, there are a million ways to celebrate.

It's easy to get bogged down in the middle of a project. It's easy to worry or receive rejection. But part of the joy of writing can and should be celebrating success— whether it's big or only big to us.

Scripture

Shout for joy to the Lord, all the earth, burst into jubilant song with music (Psalm 98:4).

Prayer

Dear Jesus, thank you for being with us during the writing process. Thank you for giving us this moment to pause and celebrate.

We recognize that often our projects feel like they have no end in sight; that maybe we'll never finish them. But we know that you are with us in the process. That alone is reason to celebrate.

Please still our minds throughout our writing lives and remind us that you are the reason to celebrate and that you celebrate along with us when we are writing to bring you honor. Amen.

Notes, Questions & Prompts

What part of the writing process can I be grateful for today?

What writing achievement can I celebrate?

Who can I share my celebration with?

With whom can I help celebrate their success?

Marketing & Promotion

If we have created a work we believe in, we have a responsibility to see that the people who need to read what we have written can find it. Marketing and promotion and branding is not a matter of pride. It is a matter of having a ministry—seeing to the needs of others by offering them what you have created.

Rather than being a source of self-importance and vanity, the process of marketing and promotion can make a person humble and modest. It is a matter of putting yourself out into the world for all to see.

Scripture

~

"You are the light of the world. A town built on a hill cannot be hidden. Neither do people light a lamp and put it under a bowl. Instead they put it on its stand, and it gives light to everyone in the house." (Matthew 5:14-16).

Prayer

Heavenly Father, we know you value humility in your children. We want to be humble; especially in our writing. Yet we also want our work to be read by the readers for whom we write.

Please help us understand the difference between humility and knowing the value of what we have produced. Help us remember that even if one person is affected for the better by our words, it is worth the effort in getting those words to them. Help us not hide our work but get them into the world so that they may light the way to you. Amen.

Notes, Questions & Prompts

What is the specific value of each of my writing pieces?

What is the specific audience for each of my writing pieces?

Is there a niche market or specific location where there would be interest for any of my pieces?

What I want to remember about this writing issue:

Branding

When we write as a career, we intend to create a body of work. That body of work hopefully finds readers who appreciate what we write and want to read more of it. As part of letting the world know about us and our writing, we seek to establish a brand—a way we can be found and recognized amid the other writers in the world.

Scripture

~

In the same way, let your light shine before others, that they may see your good deeds and glorify your Father in heaven (Matthew 5:16).

Prayer

Dear Jesus, when we are working on branding ourselves as writers, please help us find clarity. Please give us insight into how you see us as your child.

Help us use that vision to share with the world; not for our glory, but so that others might see your light shining through us. Amen.

Notes, Questions & Prompts

Do I understand what it is to have a brand? Where can I go to learn about it?

Do I have a clear understanding of how I want to be seen?

What is the mission statement for my writing?

Do I have an online presence? If so, what should I be doing that I'm not?

If not, should I have one? What first step can I take?

What I want to remember about this writing issue:

Public Speaking

~

We writers use words to inspire, educate and entertain. Usually those words are written and read by others. Sometimes though they are spoken. Speaking to groups of readers is one way to get our message out to those who need to hear it.

Although many people fear public speaking, it is always an opportunity—not to be missed—to share our creations with the world.

Scripture

~

"Now go; I will help you speak and will teach you what to say" (Exodus 4:12).

Prayer

~

Dear Jesus, it is one thing for us to sit quietly in a corner and write out our thoughts. It's something completely different for us to stand in front of an audience and speak boldly.

Please remind us that you want us to be your hands and feet in this world. Being your hands can mean stringing words together on a page. But being your feet involves going and standing. Please help us stand firm when you give us the opportunity to do so in front of other people, with confidence and assurance that you are standing there with us. Amen.

Notes, Questions & Prompts

Am I willing to do public speaking in a large group setting?

Am I willing to speak informally before small groups?

If I were to speak, what topic would be appropriate for me?

What groups might I approach about speaking to them?

What I want to remember about this writing issue:

Giving Back

When we first begin writing, we often feel lost and alone, even amid the joy of writing. During those times, often someone will come alongside us to encourage us, teach us or share their experience in a way that moves us forward in our craft.

What a privilege and honor it is when we can come alongside someone else to encourage, teach or share with them part of our own writing journey.

Scripture

~

Give, and it will be given to you. A good measure, pressed down, shaken together and running over, will be poured into your lap. For with the measure you use, it will be measured to you (Luke 6:38).

Prayer

~

Dear Jesus, please remind us that we are not to horde our talent, but that we are to share it with others. Not only are we to get our writing out to readers but we are also to share our understanding of the writing craft with other writers who may be struggling to learn.

Please also remind us, Holy Spirit of the many times you encouraged us through your leading and presence. Remind us of the people who prayed over our writing and those who came alongside us to guide and encourage us. Help us use those experiences to encourage others. Please also remind us that the author's name on the cover of the book is not as important as the fact that you are inside and are part of the process. Amen.

Notes, Questions & Prompts

What three lessons have I learned about writing that I could share with others?

Is there a specific person I could mentor?

Is there an article, blog post or book I could write to help others based on my personal experience or knowledge?

Is there someone who has mentored me that I need to thank today?

What I want to remember about this writing issue:

Further Encouragement

~

You may discover other parts of the writing process that are difficult for you. If one is not included here, just remember the model. Place your bottom in the chair and pray. Then write.

Here are some additional writing-related scripture.

~

Writing in Obedience to God's Call

Your word is a lamp for my feet, a light on my path (Psalm 119:105).

Further Encouragement

Commit to the Lord *whatever you do, and he will establish your plans* (Proverbs 16:3).

That each of them may eat and drink, and find satisfaction in all their toil—this is the gift of God (Ecclesiastes 3:13).

I urge you to live a life worthy of the calling you have received. Be completely humble and gentle; be patient, bearing with one another in love (Ephesians 4:1-2).

Dear friends, although I was very eager to write to you about the salvation we share, I felt compelled to write and urge you to contend for the faith that was once for all entrusted to God's holy people (Jude 1:3).

This calls for patient endurance on the part of the people of God who keep his commands and remain faithful to Jesus (Revelation 14:12).

Do your best to present yourself to God as one approved, a worker who does not need to be ashamed and who correctly handles the word of truth (2 Timothy 2:15).

All Scripture is God-breathed and is useful for teaching, rebuking, correcting and training in righteousness, so that the servant of God may be thoroughly equipped for every good work (2 Timothy 3:16-17).

Let us not become conceited, provoking and envying each other (Galatians 5:26).

But the Advocate, the Holy Spirit, whom the Father will send in my name, will teach you all things and will remind you of everything I have said to you (John 14:26).

In the beginning was the Word, and the Word was with God, and the Word was God (John 1:1).

Whatever you do, work at it with all your heart, as working for the Lord, not for human masters (Colossians 3:23).

Words have Power

Heaven and earth will pass away, but my words will never pass away (Matthew 24:35).

For the word of God is alive and active. Sharper than any double-edged sword, it penetrates even to dividing soul and spirit, joints and marrow; it judges the thoughts and attitudes of the heart (Hebrews 4:12).

"If you utter what is precious, and not what is worthless, you shall be as my mouth" (Jeremiah 15:19).

113

Non-Fiction Writing

"For by your words you will be acquitted, and by your words you will be condemned" (Matthew 12:37).

Let your conversation be always full of grace, seasoned with salt, so that you may know how to answer everyone (Colossians 4:6).

Let no one deceive you with empty words, for because of such things God's wrath comes on those who are disobedient (Ephesians 5:6).

At the beginning their words are folly; at the end they are wicked madness—and fools multiply words (Ecclesiastes 10:13-14).

Not many of you should become teachers, my fellow believers, because you know that we who teach will be judged more strictly (James 3:1).

A person finds joy in giving an apt reply—and how good is a timely word (Proverbs 15:23).

But when he, the Spirit of truth, comes, he will guide you into all the truth. He will not speak on his own; he will speak only what he hears, and he will tell you what is yet to come (John 16:13).

Inspirational Writing

Gracious words are a honeycomb, sweet to the soul and healing to the bones (Proverbs 16:24).

The Spirit gives life; the flesh counts for nothing. The words I have spoken to you—they are full of the Spirit and life (John 6:63).

Finally, brothers and sisters, whatever is true, whatever is noble, whatever is right, whatever is pure, whatever is lovely, whatever is admirable—if anything is excellent or praiseworthy—think about such things (Philippians 4:8).

Story

Jesus spoke to them again in parables... (Matthew 22:1-14).

No one knows what is coming—who can tell someone else what will happen after them? (Ecclesiastes 10:13-14).

so is my word that goes out from my mouth: It will not return to me empty, but will accomplish what I desire and achieve the purpose for which I sent it (Isaiah 55:11).

Rejection

a time to weep and a time to laugh, a time to mourn and a time to dance (Ecclesiastes 3:4).

but those who hope in the Lord will renew their strength. they will soar on wings like eagles; they will run and not grow weary, they will walk and not be faint (Isaiah 40:31).

For I know the plans I have for you," declares the Lord, "plans to prosper you and not to harm you, plans to give you hope and a future (Jeremiah 29:11).

Yet this I call to mind and therefore I have hope: Because of the Lord's great love we are not consumed, for his compassions never fail. They are new every morning; great is your faithfulness. I say to myself, "The Lord is my portion; therefore I will wait for him." The Lord is good to those whose hope is in him, to the one who seeks him (Lamentations 3:21-25).

Have I not commanded you? Be strong and courageous. Do not be afraid; do not be discouraged, for the Lord your God will be with you wherever you go" (Joshua 1:9).

What, then, shall we say in response to these things? If God is for us, who can be against us? (Romans 8:31).

Writing to Honor God

May these words of my mouth and this meditation of my heart be pleasing in your sight, Lord, my Rock and my Redeemer (Psalm 19:14).

And whatever you do, whether in word or deed, do it all in the name of the Lord Jesus, giving thanks to God the Father through him (Colossians 3:17).

Let the message of Christ dwell among you richly as you teach and admonish one another with all wisdom through psalms, hymns, and songs from the Spirit, singing to God with gratitude in your hearts (Colossians 3:16).

But I tell you that everyone will have to give account on the day of judgment for every empty word they have spoken (Matthew 12:36).

And we know that in all things God works for the good of those who love him, who have been called according to his purpose (Romans 8:28).

Do nothing out of selfish ambition or vain conceit. Rather, in humility value others above yourselves, not looking to your own interests but each of you to the interests of the others (Philippians 2:3-4).

Revision

Do you see someone who speaks in haste? There is more hope for a fool than for them (Proverbs 29:20).

Sin is not ended by multiplying words, but the prudent hold their tongues (Proverbs 10:19).

"How long will you say such things? Your words are a blustering wind (Job 8:2).

being confident of this, that he who began a good work in you will carry it on to completion until the day of Christ Jesus (Philippians 1:6).

I can do all this through him who gives me strength (Philippians 4:13).

Networking

"For where two or three gather in my name, there am I with them" (Matthew 18:20).

Your love has given me great joy and encouragement, because you, brother, have refreshed the hearts of the Lord's people (Philemon 1:7).

Author's Thanks

Thank you for reading this book and thank you for answering Jesus' call to write. I continue to pray for all of God's children of faith who write in obedience to Him, in a way that honors Him and points others to Him.

Please go to my website www.carolpetersonauthor.com for more ways to pray for others and for articles on faith and the craft of writing. Know that I will be praying for you and your writing as together we write in obedience to Him.

If you found this book helpful, I would appreciate it if you could go to Amazon.com, click on the link to this book, and leave a short review. Maybe your review could help another author! Thank you.

Books by Carol Peterson

From Honor Bound Books

Writer's Book Shelf series:

- *The Praying Writer: Prayers & Scripture for the Writing Process*
- *The Write Brand: Becoming Known in the World*
- *Working Together; Achieving Success: Critiquing, Marketing, Masterminds*
- *Writers as Entrepreneurs: It's Your Business*

With Faith Like Hers Bible Study Series: Studies on the character and circumstances of women in Scripture. Books available or coming soon:

- *I am Eve*
- *I am Esther*
- *I am Ruth*
- *I am Mary*
- *I am Elizabeth*
- *I am Rahab*

- *I am Hannah*
- *I am Deborah*

- *Flowers, Gemstones & Jesus: Finding Jesus in the Months of the Year*
- *Rebuild Your Tattered Temple: Small Toward Better Health*

From Mustard Seed Books (an imprint of Honor Bound Books) for children:

- *Counting Blessings* (Picture Book)
- *You and Me at the Sea* (Picture Book)
- *Stealing Sunlight: Bernie of Belleterre Book 1* (Middle Grade Novel)
- *Hydro Phobia: Bernie of Belleterre Book 2* (Middle Grade Novel)

From Libraries Unlimited

- *Fun with Finance: Math + Literacy = $uccess* (2009)
- *Jump into Science: Themed Science Fairs* (2007)
- *Around the World Through Holidays: Cross-Curricular Readers Theatre* (2005)
- *Jump Back in Time: A Living History Resource* (2004)

About the Author

Carol writes to inspire, educate and entertain. Her focus is sharing God's love with the world through a study of Scripture and opening other's eyes to see evidence of Jesus in the world around them—especially kids.

Carol is an operating director with Idaho Creative Authors Network (ICAN), helping writers learn to write, publish, and market their work.

You can find her online at her website www.CarolPetersonAuthor.com where she posts about faith.

www.ingramcontent.com/pod-product-compliance
Lightning Source LLC
Chambersburg PA
CBHW061736020426
42331CB00006B/1252